WOULD YOU LIKE SOME Salad WITH YOUR Ranch?

KELSEY PIERCHOSKI

WOULD YOU LIKE SOME Salad WITH YOUR Ranch?

A SNARKY
SERVER'S
GUIDE

HOW TO SURVIVE THE CUSTOMERS, THE COWORKERS,
THE KITCHEN, AND THE MANAGERS

WOULD YOU LIKE SOME SALAD WITH YOUR
RANCH?

Published by Park Harwich Press in Latrobe, Pennsylvania. All
rights reserved.

10 9 8 7 6 5 4 3 2 1

Library of Congress Control Number: 2019910992

Cover design by and graphics courtesy of K-Lee Gaffney
Back cover photo by Brittany Lee Photography

Print ISBN: 978-0-578-55444-0
Ebook ISBN: 978-0-578-55445-7

PUBLISHER'S NOTE: Names have been changed to protect
the identity and privacy of individuals described herein.

PARK
HARWICH
PRESS

This book is dedicated to my incredible parents, Donna and Eric Pierchoski, for believing in me to do anything, and to Renee Stallings, whose guidance and fostering brought me out as a writer.

Acknowledgments

First and foremost, thank you to my Lord and Savior Jesus Christ and my parents for whatever talents I might have, the nurturing of them, and the eternal support in achieving my goals.

Thank you to my graphic designer K-Lee Gaffney for making this book pop with your beautiful work. You did a phenomenal job.

I owe a huge debt of gratitude to my accomplished and talented friend Mark Brewer. You've been my publishing guardian angel. Thank you for taking me under your wing since we first met. Thank you for your artistic perspective and wise advice. I would've been a lot more lost without your selfless guidance, and I'm so glad to call you a friend. I'll pay it forward.

J.C. Rodgers, you were the first person to urge me to turn my short notes and diary entries about this craziness into a book by saying, "I'd buy that." Thank you for that.

Thanks to my long-time friend Joe Sacchetti. Your excitement and encouragement about this project was so appreciated, from the first few ideas to the final product. I'm so glad Mrs. Pompelia put us together in chem all those years ago.

To my various friends and coworkers who read excerpts, provided feedback, and refueled me to keep going, thank you.

Thank you to the man who hired me for this job, and the management that kept me there. Without you, so many of my dreams wouldn't have come true. The money took me through college and quite literally around the world – 26 countries so far. Thank you for helping make it happen.

Much appreciation to each of the very real customers I encountered who created the scenarios in these pages. You all played your part in crafting this story, and in fostering my sense of humor, and for that I am grateful. Without all the unpleasant stuff, I wouldn't have had anything to write.

Last but certainly not least, a million thanks to the coworkers who I spent almost six years of my life with. We endured some crap, and we had some fun. Thank you for all the inside jokes, hysterical laughter, and shared meals. Thanks for never throwing out my giant salad-in-a-mixing-bowl that I took four hours to eat, and for laughing at my snarky mouth. It was a crazy ride. Thanks for the memories, and the material.

Foreword

When Kelsey asked me to write the foreword to *Would You Like Some Salad with Your Ranch?*, I was so excited to have the honor. Not just because of my restaurant background, but because of my admiration and respect for the author. I have known Kelsey since we were 16, although it wasn't until a few years later that she became one of my true friends.

During my restaurant years, when I was spinning pizza dough, whipping up sauces, and trying to keep the line cooks under my command from burning everything we sold, Kelsey was in the front of the house, taking notes and keeping score of all the madness: poised, calm, and in control, often with an eyebrow raised and a smirk on her lips.

While I and almost everyone else I knew in the industry were out late after every shift, drowning our life sorrows and job misery in alcohol and weed, thinking we were the epitome of cool, Kelsey was home, lounging in a bathrobe, sipping a responsible cup of tea, turning the experiences we so detested into the hilarity you hold in your hands.

From my perspective, she's someone who has the maturity and vision to take a circumstance, especially one you're not always happy about, and flip it on its head to something that's funny, enjoyable, relatable, and even profitable. Where I and others said, *I hate this*, Kelsey said, *I can write about this*. She's a passionate and engaging writer who captured and held my attention throughout this book, and she has a true gift for storytelling in a way that's relevant. She nailed all the elements of restaurant work that servers have to deal with, and gave me a fresh respect for how hard it is to deal with both the front and back of the house simultaneously.

Kels is, and always has been, one of my role models for drive, ambition, and delivery – she's always been all action and all hands on deck to achieve her goals.

I have truly loved reading this new book of Kelsey's that you hold in your hand, maybe with your drink of choice after a hard shift in the other. So may I make a toast! To

Kelsey! Creative, visionary, comedian, and queen of sassiness!

Long may you write!

J. S.

Former pizza cook, sous chef master, line cook, and all-around kitchen confidant

Contents

IV *Keeping Up with The Kitchen*
Creepy. Cute. Crazy.

V *Managing the Managers*
Don't bite the hand that feeds you

Introduction

I never pictured myself in the food industry. At all. Touching other people's dirty silverware (sans gloves) and wearing the same uniform (unwashed) for days in a row wasn't my idea of a desirable job.

Then college came and after a break-up I found myself free on the weekends and in need of money. After a short-lived stint working retail, I thought I'd rather die a slow and painful death than stand behind another cash register or rearrange another shelf display. So I decided to try something new and applied to a few restaurants.

I got a job as a busser at a local chain in 2010 and made tips for the first time in my life. I liked the ever-changing nature of the job. No two days were the same, and I never knew how much money I could walk out with. I was motivated, and it became a game on a number of levels. How well can you keep up? How much chaos can you handle? How well can you multi-task? How much money can you make? I enjoyed the fast-paced, on-your-feet atmosphere, dirty uniform and sweaty body and flirty kitchen boys and all.

In early 2012, I got the serving job I had until late 2017. It carried me through half of college, buying my first nice car, an engagement and impending wedding, the financial fall out of those plans being dashed, and numerous travels and expensive purchases. It was both my full-time job while I searched for a position within my field of study and a part-time cushion for extra cash. It was a place where I met great friends and not so great guys. It was the job that taught me about people, about money, and about hard work.

In this book you will find four sections of the service industry, each comprised of stereotypical types of people working in most establishments. Of course, I couldn't cover everyone – you'll have to handle the clingy weird girl attached to your hip and the girl who cries in the bathroom every shift from being overwhelmed without my help.

All of the situations, events, people, and quotes you are about to encounter are 100% real, first-hand experiences I've had. As anyone who works in the service industry knows, you can't make this stuff up.

So whether you work in a 5-star pad or a basic dive bar, I hope you find something in this book that strikes a chord with you. Something that makes you laugh, roll your eyes in understanding, or grit your teeth and scream, "Yes! That's exactly how it is!"

No matter how you feel about your current station in life, whether you love serving or are desperate to get out of it, I hope you put your feet up, relax, and find some little bits of humor in these pages. Just don't read too much before bed, or those nightmares of handling a rush alone or flashbacks of never getting that ranch for table 21 might start again.

Your First Shift

What could go wrong?

My first night post-training, I got a chaotic table of young college students and romantic vibes from one of the girls. She left me her phone number along with a wink. It was a great way to begin. Or not.

The next day, my only mistake was forgetting to give a customer a pen to sign their credit card slip. That was quickly overridden by the fact that during a busy Saturday lunch shift, I hadn't noticed a new table, naively thinking the hosts would actually tell you when you were seated, and I took way too long to greet them. Then I forgot to ring in their order.

One of my new coworkers exploded, "You HAVE to WATCH your SECTION!"

The boss told me that would be counted as my one allotted major mistake.

It could only be up from there, right?

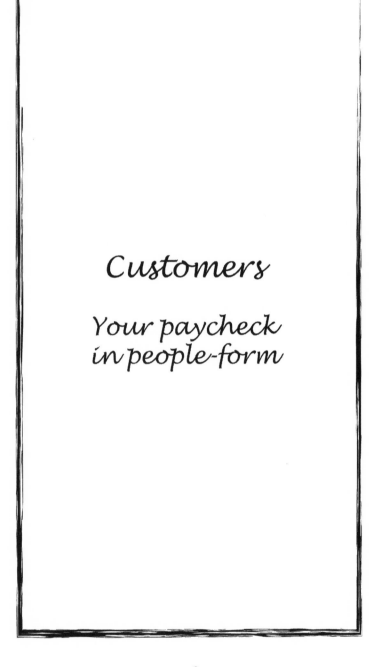

Customers

Your paycheck
in people-form

That Couple with the Baby

I always particularly enjoyed waiting on kids as a sort of mock trial run to having them. You learn as much about the parenting styles as you do about kids themselves. Which parent are you, or which will you aspire to be?

The one who patiently reads off every choice of drink, prompts their angel with two or three choices, then waits for five excruciating minutes for their princess to select one? Finally, after some incoherent babble, the parent orders for the child like they should have in the first place.

Or what about the parent who encourages creative play with the sugar packets, salt, ketchup, and ranch dressing?

The one who lets their kids practice their aim by throwing the animal crackers, crayons, and remnants of gooey food brought from home?

What about the parents who let their child get their cardio in by running, crawling, and screaming through the restaurant, tripping you and disturbing everyone in the process?

I think my favorite is the parent who does all of the above, then leaves you a 15% tip for cleaning up the remains of a daycare where you don't work.

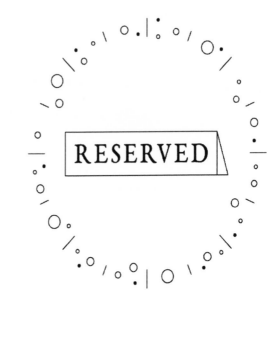

The Regulars

Regulars. Thorn in your side or saving grace? Do they morph back and forth?

There was the "Bonnet Lady," or Jane once I learned her name, who always stumbled in and sat herself in a booth in the bar. She ordered Johnny Walker Black Label shots on the rocks and occasionally some food that when delivered, she'd say she didn't order. Everyone really got concerned when she thought it was October in the middle of June. Eventually I learned that her family flew in and put her in a nursing home because she'd gotten too confused to live alone. I hoped someone occasionally smuggled in some Johnny.

There was my generic family who chugged Coors Light, always had their scrubs on, and never had anything new to say.

The bar regulars were household names with the staff: the Iced Tea Man, the bikers, Luke who rode out to Sturgis every summer, and the 50 year-old death metal lovers who shouted, screamed, went behind the bar, hogged the jukebox, and generally drove away the decent paying customers.

My true favorite regulars were Ben and his friend, Leo. Almost every UFC fight night I could count on them to come in and make it worthwhile. Ben was a hardworking truck driver with no shortage of job-hunting wisdom to impart on me in my seemingly endless years of post-college purgatory.

"Don't let them pile more responsibilities on you with no increase in pay. You can't do the work of three people for the pay of one."

Feel familiar?

The Alcohol Taste-Testers (and plain old alcoholics)

Ahh, the alcohol taste-testers and self-appointed experts who yet still don't seem to know what they're ordering. Surely you're qualified to explain every beer's hop level, amount of head, color, and flavor to them, even though you barely drink, or don't drink beer. Of course you know every drink's full ingredient list and amount of each. You don't have anything else to remember, do you? You're required to have the knowledge of a 5-star bartender in both a hot NYC nightclub and a local pub featuring seasonal brews.

There should be a name for the specific anger you feel after fetching five samples of obscure beers only to hear, "I'll just take a Bud."

You can't talk about alcohol without talking about the alcoholics. Or at least, people who seem like they would be, since they can polish off six 22 oz. glasses of beer and act stone cold sober. And to everyone who orders complicated drinks and the server tries to tell you they don't have the precise ingredients, but you still order anyway and then claim they taste

"weird," well, that's because we don't have blueberry vodka.

We have blueberry schnapps, as I explained to you beforehand.

The dialog with these people is always a pure pleasure.

"Can you tell them light ice?"

Because that means more alcohol?

"It doesn't taste right."

What doesn't taste right about a rum and Coke?

"It's not very strong."

Uh, I don't know, I watched the bartenders pour and

they measured each shot correctly, so that's on you.

I think perhaps my favorite experience was the group

of 12 college kids (here we go again) of whom only one was a

true nightmare. His off-kilter attempt at sitting down revealed

his intoxication level, but in case there was any doubt, he loudly

proclaimed how buzzed he was to the entire table. No shock

then about his attitude when I asked for his I.D., which of

course he didn't have. The walk out to the car for I.D.

produced a piece of paper that's kind of like a temporary

driver's license. In my opinion we shouldn't have accepted that, but my shift supervisor let it slide.

The kid tried to order triples. I told him no. He tried to order three drinks at once. That's not our policy. I gave him two instead. He tried to order complicated stuff I didn't know how to ring in. It all went on for hours and ended in my supervisor and I cutting him off.

He wrote an e-mail to corporate trying to get us both fired. Our district manager laughed at it and congratulated us on doing the right thing.

Yes, that guy had since returned.

No, I wouldn't wait on him.

The Tourists

My area doesn't get a lot of tourism, but the tourists always unwittingly gave themselves away by their butchered pronunciations of our local fare, regional cuisines, and specialty drinks named after sports icons. The frequent use of Native American and German names for towns and bodies of water didn't help matters much, either.

Giving advice to out-of-towners for "cool" things to do, when you consider your area to be interesting only to a 70-year-old Revolutionary War enthusiast, was always a fun challenge. There's a path in a park you could walk, or maybe you want to attend a concert of a washed-up 1970's rock band?

The choices were limitless, but believe it or not, I fared far better giving directions. When customers reappeared in the restaurant 30 minutes later and I heard them asking someone else for the same directions, I was sure they just hadn't been listening closely enough.

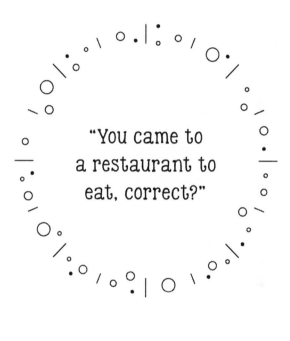

"You came to
a restaurant to
eat, correct?"

*-a blunt coworker, about a table
taking too long to order*

Indecisive Decision-makers

Of all the frustrating and trying things about being a server, this one is a definite contender for most irritating. When I give you ample time to peruse the menu, and you require three more stretches of time, and I come back to the signal that you're ready but then it turns out you're really not, well, that's just annoying.

"We're ready" doesn't mean you continue to stare blankly at the menu.

It doesn't mean you order and second-guess yourself.

It doesn't mean you order and then ask five questions about three other items, waffling back and forth between other choices.

And it doesn't mean playing musical chairs about who is going to start ordering, as if someone in your party is going to have lifelong emotional wounds from not ordering first.

"We're ready" means you order concisely and efficiently, because your server has 20 other things they need to do.

The Rude People

I think all the books in the world couldn't contain the stories of rude, ignorant, obnoxious jerks that seem to be out to ruin your night and make you hate your job.

People who loudly demand silverware for everything from wings to French fries, complain nonstop about everything from the temperature to the TV's, or throw a fit when they can't sit at the "perfect" table.

People who patronize and talk down to you, ask personal questions, or demand to speak to a manager about a non-issue or one you've already satisfactorily resolved.

People who eat their whole meal and then want a new one, and/or want it for free.

People who communicate more with their phones than with you.

People who cut you off mid-greeting with "Water with lemon."

People who study the menu to ask you in-depth, crazily detailed questions you couldn't possibly know the answer to, just to make you look stupid.

"Why don't you have (insert brand name here) crumbled bleu cheese?"

Maybe because bleu cheese is revolting and nobody wants it.

"What's in your house dressing?"

Does the menu say we even have one? No? Then we don't.

"Where does your meat come from?"

Uh, some frozen warehouse somewhere, I guess. Did you think we specially butchered it and smoked it in the private smokehouse out back just for you?

Of course, you can't leave this category without touching the elephant in the room – people who tip like crap, or who dare not tip at all. Servers aren't serving for the fun of it, or for volunteer points on their resume. We have lives and bills and expenses like everyone else, and if you're not okay with tipping appropriately, then do everyone a favor and stay home.

People who Tip Really Well

This is where I say a heartfelt thank you to every patron who tips well, even when the server might be having an off or bad day, or when you're feeling grouchy, or just didn't like things that much.

Thank you for making our day and our night worth it. People like you are the reason we do this job and (sometimes) love it.

Without the good tips of many great customers, I wouldn't have been able to succeed in as many ways, so from the bottom of my heart, thank you.

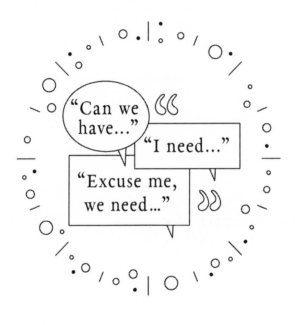

Needy Whiners

Another all too common nuisance in the serving world are the people who think they're the only ones in the restaurant, and you are to accommodate them as such.

Symptoms of this kind of customer are: asking for extra of everything (and it's usually already on the table), needing six refills, asking for to-go boxes, bags, drinks, and lids (all at different times), and needing something every time you so much as look in their direction. You usually make anywhere from three to six trips for this table, and the tip doesn't reflect that. Bonus points on the neediness scale if all of those trips could've been combined into one.

The only positive I can think of is that you're getting in your steps. In my entire serving career I meant to wear a pedometer just once out of curiosity, but the achy legs at the end of a shift told me enough.

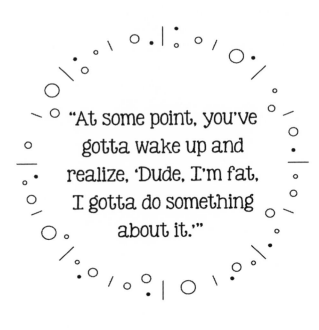

"At some point, you've gotta wake up and realize, 'Dude, I'm fat, I gotta do something about it.'"

-a brutally honest coworker

Professional Eaters

Every once in awhile you get a table that blows your mind with how much food they order. I can eat as much as the next person, and usually more, if my ex-boyfriends were any indication. But this is the kind of compulsive ordering that causes dollar signs to light up in your eyes as you listen, gaping, to the order that goes on with no end in sight.

Two signature mixed drinks, a colossal plate of loaded nachos, onion rings, and a side of cheese fries drizzled with ranch dressing and bacon started things off strong. A half-pound cheeseburger with fries, a side of five chicken wings, and a heaping grilled chicken salad topped with fries and side of chili with cheese and onions followed.

A gigantic brownie sundae capped off the evening, along with coffees and a slice of pecan pie to go.

This was a table of two.

People with a Special Diet

I'm not discounting those that have a serious allergy or food intolerance, however strange and uncommon it might be (lemons or olives, anyone?).

However, we all know people who jumped on the gluten-free bandwagon or those who have no logic to their needs, which seem to only be in place to make your job harder.

I once had a customer ask for no cheese on a burger because of a "dairy allergy," then order ice cream for dessert. Also included in this category are those that bring their own drink or order an item but modify it beyond recognition.

My hands down favorite offender was the woman who would always order the same salad, consistently asking me to take half of the veggies out and substitute different ones, all in different amounts, to make sure none of them touched each other, and that her dressing cup on the side didn't touch the plate.

She also brought her own water.

Big Parties

A lot of the success or pain of this category is dependent upon the rules of your establishment and the type of party it is. Where I worked, literally anything goes. We had a "split parties of 12 or more" policy, which nobody followed once they got to be a strong server and could handle more and more pandemonium solo.

I've had upwards of 30 at one table, ranging from family reunions to birthday parties to sports teams. Sometimes it was blessedly easy, with one leader ordering pizzas and Coke for everyone, but more often, it was a true test of my organizational, listening, and memorization skills as I tried to match faces with orders and physical descriptions with seats. Throw in a loud sporting event on TV and all separate checks and you can already feel your heart rate increasing.

Adding to the chaos was the extra clutter of balloons, gift bags, and cupcakes, all getting in the way as I tried to maneuver around excited, chatty people who hadn't seen each other in awhile. Cleaning up the aftermath and fishing for every last dollar bill amid the cold leftovers and smeared icing usually took place in stages over the course of an hour.

The real kicker? My restaurant was stuck in the Dark Ages as far as their auto-gratuity policy, which was nonexistent. That's correct. No auto-gratuity, on any size party. By some stroke of luck, or possibly I actually did a good job, I always seemed to do okay.

I hope you have more of the straightforward, peaceful parties and fewer of the ones that cause cold sweats and panic attacks.

Sports People

These characters come in all shapes and sizes, from families and couples to whole fraternities, shouting and whooping and knocking chairs over in their enthusiasm. Where I worked, the NHL was the star attraction. Except for the UFC fight nights, which brought out the grimiest, grittiest people in society, filling every table in overwhelming numbers and staying for five hours while leaving four dollars, if they left anything at all. I remember chasing one couple outside with a manager after they walked out on their check and dragging them back to pay.

A good time was had by all.

Waiting on sports people, although an extremely long process because they camp in your section for hours, was usually simple, because they ordered beer, pizza, and wings, or some combination thereof. You really need to shine in your recognition skills for these folks though, because 10 people all dressed in the same two colors and variations of the same jersey is trying to the memory like nothing else.

Although usually friendly, albeit a tad clueless, these people always elicited an extreme eye-roll from me because first of all, does this game really mean that much to you in your personal life?

And second, do you really expect anyone to appreciate the way you, a mid-forties, overweight, balding guy wearing a Fitbit looks in that jersey, instead of the toned, muscular 28 year-old professional athlete it really belongs to?

Campers

This is a definite contender for all-time most infuriating thing you can do to your server.

For every table that follows the natural beat of the dining out experience, i.e. order, eat, pay, leave, there unfortunately seems to be one who thinks it goes something like this: order, eat, wait two hours to pay, pay, sit for another hour, order a cup of coffee, pay again, sit again, and finally, as you're sweeping the floor and turning off the lights, leave.

I can't for the life of me fathom why some people have no sense of social cues (me standing in the corner staring you down, me walking by the table, me asking you consistently if there's anything else I can do for you), or understanding of the fact that a restaurant is a business, not your living room.

Server's sections are their real estate they're renting out to you for your meal, and maybe a little bit of chit-chat, but no longer. If you're going to sit for the length of time it would've taken three other tables to eat and leave, then you need to tip enough to cover those three tables your server missed out on having.

Can't do that? Then don't hang around.

You wouldn't let someone live in your home for free when you could get a tenant that pays rent, now would you?

I always let my imagination drift when it came to campers.

Why do they have to sit here, in a loud, crowded restaurant, at a sticky table, to talk?

Are they homeless?

Don't they have somewhere they could go that's more comfortable and conducive to private conversation?

Do they really like being here that much?

If so, then maybe they can have my job.

Last but not least, the People

you Truly Enjoy

This one is dedicated to all the customers who make you smile, who elicit a laugh, who speak a kind word, or who leave a fantastic tip.

The ones who go out of their way to leave a sweet note of thanks, or who call your manager over to tell them how lucky they are to have you as an employee.

The people who are genuine and pleasant enough to make you want to stay and talk more than you have to, or who make you feel comfortable enough to drop your fake server voice.

Thank you, thank you, and thank you. Please keep coming back, and make sure you ask for me.

Coworkers

The thorn in your other side

"Can someone take
my first table?
My nails aren't dry yet."

- a very high maintenance server

The Bombshell

I worked with a girl who spent so much time and energy becoming physically perfect that it was hard to stop staring at her. I never wanted her to think I was just as big of a creep as the guys in the kitchen though, because all I wanted to do was copy her perfect smoky eyes and angled contouring.

Maybe you've worked with somebody like this.

Somebody with sleek hair that never rumples during a shift, impeccable make-up, an atomically correct body compliments of a plastic surgeon, a freshly laundered uniform, and shiny lacquered acrylic nails, accentuating the rock so huge on her left ring finger that she was in danger of sinking if she stepped in a swimming pool.

To make me feel even more inferior, this girl was only a couple years older than me and so nice, sweet, and soft-spoken amid the stress of the customer service industry that I thought she actually might be an angel.

"Kels, what should
I eat for lunch?
I need carbs.
I'm drinking later."

-one of the best partiers at work

The 4th Kardashian Sister

In the same vein as the beauty above is this girl, who was the world's best quick-change artist.

Coming into work in her pajamas, she would emerge from the bathroom only minutes later, cleavage popping out, black hair silky straight, and a face ready for a full night hitting the clubs.

I used to spend a lot of time wondering how she could stand working in clothes so tight they looked painted on, how much money she spent on her daily tanning habit, and why she thought I was a good person to help her prep for her long nights out partying.

She never took my suggestions.

"Has anyone
seen my milk?"

- *an awkward coworker*

Awkward Girl

This is a role that I lavished in playing myself occasionally, but more often than not, my coworker more than picked up the slack.

Her true shining moment was greeting a table while her apron slowly fell down around her ankles as she talked. I wasn't lucky enough to witness this hilarity, but can still feel wells of laughter bubbling up inside me at the very thought of it.

When she wasn't talking about *Star Wars* or her civil engineering homework, one of her favorite things to do was drink a gigantic jug of milk, which she'd police with fervor, lest anyone decide to dip into her dairy obsession.

My goodness, I miss her.

"Did you put a finger
condom on that cut?"

- *the overbearing mother figure*

The Mom

This coworker is a wizard in the kitchen, bringing in all of her baked goods and latest recipe adventures.

She's always quick to offer tips for everything from sunburns to constipation, and even quicker to criticize other parenting. If I had a dollar for every sentence that started with "I'd never let my kids" or "when my kids were little," well, I wouldn't have needed to be at that serving job.

She makes you feel either judged and superfluous ("I remember when I was young and irresponsible"), or lovingly cared for. I remember when I cut off the tip of my thumb chopping tomatoes and the current mom on duty (and nurse-to-be) cleaned and wrapped my finger so well I lost feeling in it from the tightness of the gauze.

As much as I sometimes appreciated their eagerness to offer knowledge and homemade snickerdoodle cookies, I felt more like I was permanently cut off from this group, like they had crossed some gigantic chasm and I was still on the other side.

Which I guess is the truth, at least until I start baking every weekend and learn how to calm a colicky baby.

"Pick a letter!"

*- a friend during our rousing games of
Hangman on those tedious morning shifts*

Your Best Friends

Speaking of a chasm, these coworkers are the ones still on the other side with you.

Every once in a while, someone gets hired who you just click with – and isn't that the best feeling? When going to work is not just about money, but also about inside jokes, the same sense of sarcasm and humor, and hatred of the same coworkers? I can't even imagine restaurant life without shared shit-talking and private confessions of embarrassing coworker crushes.

My best friends were the coworkers with whom I've shared tables, feelings, food, advice, and drinks after work. They were the people who cheered for me in my victories and felt my frustrations.

The ones in the same life position as me.

The ones who did my hair for me.

The ones who played Hangman with me when it was slow and helped me when it wasn't.

Thank you for everything: for every single embarrassing, funny, stupid, happy, memorable moment along the journey of working together.

To my coworkers turned friends, I hope you read this and know who you are. Work would have sucked without you, so thank you.

I hope you have friends like this wherever you work.

"It's too nice outside to be here. Nobody's going to come in. We're going to be dead tonight."

- a dramatic complainer

The Dramatic Complainer

This server is like Negative Nellie or Johnny Raincloud on steroids. She doesn't even need to wait for a bad situation to start her spew of depression.

When she actually gets inside the building, it intensifies.

"I can't clock in. My pen broke. I hate that section. Can I be first cut?"

After taking two tables, she's had more than enough.

"I hate this place. I can't wait to leave. I don't make any money here. Am I cut yet?"

She finally gets another table, an eight top she can make some money on.

"Can someone take my table?"

There really is no pleasing this person. It's busy when they want it to be dead. It's dead when they want it to be busy. They make money when they don't want to and don't make money when they do want to. They complain about not being sat, then they complain when they are sat. Five minutes ago she wanted tables and now the host should know she doesn't anymore.

If you ever see this person's face climb out of it's deeply etched scowl, take note. I almost called the press the one time I saw her actually smile.

Despite all the gloom and doom, I usually got along with this type, because she's always ready to sarcastically bitch about something and agree with you over every little annoyance.

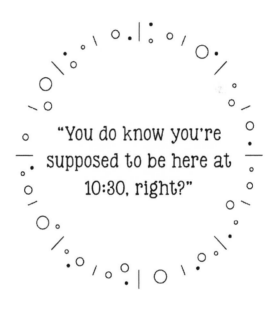

"You do know you're supposed to be here at 10:30, right?"

- a kiss-up bossypants at 10:34

61

Little Miss Bossypants

I think every establishment has this self-righteous, self-appointed representative of management that is really just another coworker.

I've worked with a few of these types, but one sticks out in my mind: the one who checked on how I was pouring chocolate syrup on a desert and offered thoughts on how I was cutting open a new bag of soup.

These people really baffle me because I can't figure out their motive.

Do you really actually care about the trivial, mundane tasks you're preaching about? Is your life that pathetic?

Do you think I need help and am too shy to ask?

Do you think you can run this place better than the manager?

Or do you really think I'm just that incompetent, needing help with everything from taking out the trash to brewing iced tea?

Last but not least, let's consider the possibility that you're just socially clueless about how to talk to others and honestly think you're being helpful.

The bossy types didn't bother me when I was new, and then when I wasn't, I just ignored them or flat out said, "I don't care" to their unsolicited advice.

This is also usually the same money-hungry person who sucks up to management, bullies everyone to get their way, sneakily changes the sections and floor chart to benefit themselves, and slyly takes extra tables, always claiming, "Oh sorry, I forgot it was your turn! You can have the next two."

Did you ever get the next two?

Thought not.

These coworkers are usually notorious for being secretly hated by everyone but are blissfully unaware, so we get the last laugh now, don't we?

"...you said
chocolate milk?"

- *a lovable but hopeless coworker,*
to a customer that clearly just ordered a Sprite

Dumber and Lazier

This is another one on which you could fill volumes.

Coworkers that ask you where a refrigerated item would be kept (hint: in the walk-in).

Coworkers that try to drain the hot water.

Coworkers that burn the soup beyond recognition because they didn't realize the soup warmers need water to heat the soup.

Coworkers that don't sweep their section, half-ass their side work, and skip out before rolling silverware. If questioned or caught, they try to pretend they forgot or didn't know they had to (not a believable tactic when you've been working here for five years, Anna).

They're usually also the whiniest, loudest, and cause the most drama. But does any of that really come as a surprise?

Just get on our level and admit you're a useless employee. We all already know.

Also falling into this category are the irresponsible flakes who consistently show up late, call off, always have an excuse why they have to leave early/can't come in/need a ride, and expect everyone else to be okay with covering their slack.

Do you really expect anyone to believe you had court, four flat tires, custody of your kid, and a seizure all in the same day?

My personal favorite was the "I fell down the stairs and hit my head excuse" used once to get out of a shift the night before the server left for vacation.

Hello, Marie? You could have just admitted you wanted to stay home and get buzzed.

We all already know that, too.

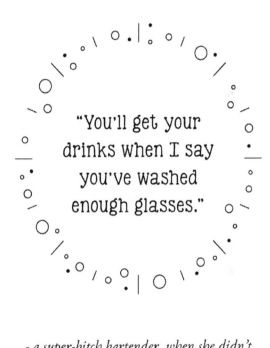

"You'll get your drinks when I say you've washed enough glasses."

- *a super-bitch bartender, when she didn't even need those glasses to make the drinks*

The Insufferably Bitchy

Bartender

When I first started my job, there was one bartender so brazenly rude to me that I thought it was hazing of some sort.

I'm talking blunt, cold, go-out-of-your-way rude. After I'd been there a few years, was proven to be competent, and saw her treating other employees the same way, I knew it was her, not me. That became my mantra for the remainder of serving my sentence having to be around this person.

Some people are just toxic and miserable. In this person's case, I knew it was that and more: she's painfully short, so I knew her attitude was an attempt to compensate for her insecurities about being the same height as a third grader.

When you're stuck working with someone who snaps at you, belittles you, yells at you, insults you in front of customers, plays games with making your drinks, and butts into your private conversations to make some rude remark, there's only one thing you do: ignore her desperate pleas for attention,

plaster on your best fake personality, play whatever game you

need to get your drinks, keep your tables happy and thus make

good money, and then turn her folly into material for this book.

Checkmate, psychopath.

"I got three hours
of sleep and I feel
like garbage, but
I passed my boards."

- *the best bartender ever, handling a busy
shift solo after finishing nursing school*

The Super Hero

On the other side of the bartender coin is the super hero, who not only defied logic by her bartending skills, but was also a kind, fun person and successful in her personal life.

The super hero bartender would always show up five minutes early, long, wavy blonde hair flowing and smelling freshly of mousse, nursing school materials in one arm and coffee in the other, ready to study between customers and making the server drinks faster than I thought possible.

Always in a good mood and happy to help, as I talked to her I learned that her model-looking husband married her after a one-night stand and brief dating stint, they had two all-American kids, and recently built a house. Soon after, she finished nursing school and got a job in a brand new hospital.

All before the age of 28.

She was "goals" in every sense of the word.

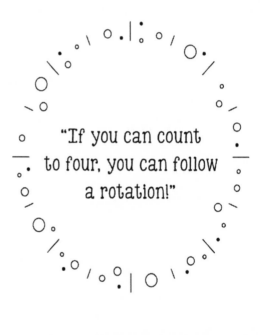

"If you can count to four, you can follow a rotation!"

- a competent host, training a hopelessly inept one

The Creepy Host

Toward the end of my employment, a host got hired who embodied "creepy" in every sense of the word.

She'd show up for work seemingly out of nowhere. I never once saw her walk in or out of the building. Her face was permanently set in an expression of dumbfounded shock, totally unreadable, black eyeliner heavily drawn around her eyes.   Her style was a mix of emo and Wal-Mart. She never spoke above a whisper, but yet never learned to talk louder when all I said to her was "what?" and "I can't hear you."

She was socially awkward, shy, scared, and completely non-confrontational. She didn't listen to any corrections nor get any better at her job. But hey, at least she didn't steal tips from tables, like the one previous host, who was the reason we got cameras.

The weirdest thing about her was that she'd come up behind you out of nowhere, get really close, and whisper "I sat you" or "you have a new table," with this coy, almost seductive smile.

Once I learned I could imitate it perfectly, I got quite a few coworkers in hysterics regularly.

"I'm too sexy
for my apron."

- an effortlessly funny guy

The Fun Dude

Thank God for this coworker who takes the edge off and lightens the mood.

The guy who bashes your cousin with you and agrees over the rudeness of her slights.

The high school guy who only talks about working out, fishing, and is "only working here to pay for my gym membership."

The guy who blasts Backstreet Boys, is always quick with a one-liner, and when he rings in something wrong, runs back to the kitchen singing "Sorry" by Justin Beiber.

The guy who brings in bags of Skittles every shift to spread around.

And then there was the Fun Dude who morphed into my crush and reason for going to work, but I'll get to that in a minute.

"You look really
beautiful tonight."

- a crush, making my night

Your Heart-Stopping Crush

You know those scenarios where people meet and butt heads, then end up being friends or even liking each other? I always thought I was too spot-on in my first impressions to ever find myself in that situation, but I was happily wrong.

At first I barely noticed the new guy who talked everyone's ear off, and I took even longer to learn his name, rolling my eyes at his loud, rambling stories and opinions.

I don't remember when or why we began interacting, but I was always curt and unfriendly with him, laughing inwardly at his constant humor but unwilling to be another girl fawning over him, offering to bake him a batch of cookies, swooning over pictures of his little daughter, or inventing a reason why he needed to rub my shoulders.

Something about my attitude must have worked, because right when I was beginning to thaw out, we went straight to outright flirting, complete with cheesy smiles, genuine compliments, and any and every opportunity to have physical contact. We became friends too, complaining and making bitchy comments about coworkers.

Serving made him flustered and easily confused, wandering in circles wasting time and getting orders wrong in the process. I still got annoyed with him sometimes, but I liked laughing and joking and him too much to ever stay genuinely mad.

After a few cowardly shifts, I got the nerve to take that huge risk where you tell a coworker (at work, no less!) you like them, and if they don't like you too, then it's going to be a whole new level of awkward.

But he said he liked me too.

He was the bright spot of every shift and the real reason I could smile about going to work. After we both quit, our friendship actually increased, and he became one of my honest-to-goodness friends.

So next time you're faced with someone who makes your face turn as red as the tomato slices, just go for it. Seriously. It might turn out wonderfully.

Keeping Up
with The Kitchen

Creepy. Cute. Crazy.

"They only let me leave to come here."

- *a cook, showing me his ankle bracelet*
and explaining the conditions of house arrest

The Felons

Every restaurant on earth must have a hiring contract with local prisons. The unsavory characters passed in and out through a revolving door, but some stood out.

There was one cook who claimed to know military-style hand-to-hand combat and to have been in a Philadelphia gang. I thought it was all just talk until he showed me the bullet wound in his torso.

Another guy covered in tattoos glared menacingly at me (and probably everyone else), screaming when I didn't do something that wasn't my job. I screamed back and he was almost friendly after that.

The one that shook me the most was an ex-con, with a record of sexual harassment, that somehow got my phone number. His girlfriend went through his phone, found it, and texted and called me nonstop for three days to the point that I turned my phone off. When I confronted him about it, he apologized, like that was supposed to be good enough.

Later that morning he was fired, and that was saying something, because my manager at the time was fully in the good ol' boys club.

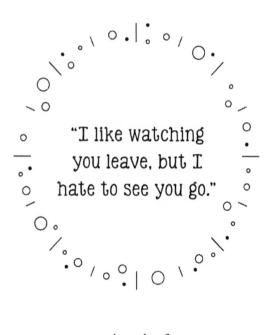

"I like watching
you leave, but I
hate to see you go."

- a shameless flirt

The Outrageously Flirty

Playboy

This cook blew me away by the sheer obviousness with which he pursued nearly every single girl for the sole purpose of having sex. Almost as astounding were the number of times he succeeded. Every time I walked around the corner, he was flirting with someone, rubbing someone's shoulders, or rattling off a compliment so sweet I felt a cavity coming on.

"And how are you today, Kelly?"

Puppy dog eyes and cheesy smile.

"Good, how are you?"

"I'm wonderful now that I get to look into those beautiful brown eyes of yours."

See what I'm saying?

Granted, he was kind of cute and funny, but that could never negate the number of STD's he probably had.

There was one girl, however, who never fell for it, and said what I was thinking every time.

"And how are you today, Jessica?"

"Why do you ask me that every day? You think the answer's ever gonna change?"

During an employee meeting, where all conscious employees know you keep quiet to avoid discussion that might prolong the pain, this guy broke the code asking pointless rhetorical questions to waste everyone's time.

This time Jessica said what we were *all* thinking.

"JUST. STOP. TALKING."

"Give me a hug,
I haven't seen
you in awhile.
Now let's go make out
in the cooler."

- a hyper-sexualized line cook

The Sexual Creeper

This ne'er-do-well takes every chance to turn a conversation sexual, makes everything into an innuendo, and/or tries to smack your butt with trays. If you complain to management, they'll probably tell you to just watch him and let them know if he does it again, upon which you and they both know they'll still do nothing.

Though usually harmless, the most unnerving run-in I had with this type was when I was only 19 and he was easily in his forties. First he was the normal amount of friendly, then it turned into asking me in-depth questions about my age, where I went to school, and incredibly, where I lived.

I lied on my feet and told the manager, and she then promptly did nothing.

I learned through the grapevine he'd been arrested for peeping in windows and breaking into someone's house. They came home to find him naked under their dining room table.

So if a guy tries to corner you in the walk-in, kiss you outside by the dumpster, smacks your butt with his bare hand, or says "let's go have sex in the cooler" and you're not feeling it, forget the managers and the bullshit protocol they operate under. Take matters into your own hands.

If all else fails, you could always strangle him with your apron strings.

"RUNNER!"

- *every cook, everywhere, every five seconds*

The Motormouths

I worked with a couple cooks who never stopped talking about anything and nothing, to nobody in particular. It didn't help that they talked fast, ran words together, and used slang foreign to my area. When I could understand them, I found myself in a cross between awe and disgust.

One maintained that, at 5'3," he was going to try out for the NBA but was too good, so he didn't want to waste his time. He also got an exemption from the physical part of the state police test. They could just tell he'd pass.

Are you laughing yet?

Another one told tall tales of participating in wild gang initiations, or at least that's what I think he was talking about. He punctured his incoherent ramblings frequently with, "you know what I'm sayin'?"

To which we'd all reply, no, we really don't know what you're saying, so please just stop.

"Dustpan, come!"

- a one-off cook, calling a dustpan like a dog

The Oddball

This cook was so incredibly out-there mentally that I imagined his thoughts as strange and uncharted as the deepest parts of the ocean – full of weird creatures you've never seen before that don't make any sense.

Unusually happy and speaking in nonsensical riddles, he once called to a dustpan and commanded it to come, like it was a dog. He'd hold a loaf of bread and play air guitar with it. When he was working, he'd often stop randomly and stare, giggling at his own thoughts, until another cook yelled at him repeatedly to sell food.

He rode his bicycle on the highway and got pulled over for a ticket only once, according to something someone said.

He used to stalk one of the bartenders, waiting outside her apartment and trying to look in her windows.

He was later seen riding around a nearby town, rocking a new look somewhere between Jesus and Forrest Gump when he runs across the country. That's the last I've heard of him.

"Jake, you know
you gotta cook both
sides of the meat, right?
You can't burn one
side and leave the
other side raw."

- a patient manager, to one of
the biggest morons going

The Dumb One

Once upon a time a cook got hired who was so mind-blowingly incompetent that when he put two pizzas in the oven, he held up four fingers to tell another cook.

When he was working, he was in slow motion. He'd stop frequently to talk, seemingly unable to speak and work simultaneously. The other cooks frequently screamed at him, but his reaction was always watered down by marijuana. He'd wander the kitchen aimlessly, moving things around and trying to look busy, until it was time to go outside and get high again. He once asked me how to spell *orange*.

No, really. This isn't stolen from *Mean Girls*.

"This wall does more work than Jake," I'd say, slapping a palm on one of the kitchen walls. "At least it holds up the building."

"Can I have
a dry shirt?"

*- a dishwasher, after fully hosing himself down
from overheating five minutes into his shift*

The Idiot Dishwasher

My restaurant was the only one I've ever worked in or heard of that didn't regularly employ a dishwasher.

There would be spurts of time with one, spurts without one. With no dishwasher, it was our problem to make sure there were enough clean dishes and silverware. Many a night we were frantically hand washing salad bowls as a table's order was coming up, and messily rolling sets of silverware as food was going out.

Such was the epic game of multi-tasking and time-keeping that we all played many a busy Saturday night.

The dishwasher working when I left fell into the woefully incompetent category. Dishes were routinely put away dirty, with smears and food particles, and suddenly it became the server's job to hunt through stacks of plates to find a clean one, while their table waited.

He refused to put cups away.

He didn't wash silverware unless pestered.

In between playing games on his phone, aimless wandering around the kitchen, and flirting with uninterested servers, he might wash a few more racks of dishes, while 50 more just piled up, until he was allowed to leave early because he's "winded."

One of his favorite tricks for curing his exhaustion after a long 30 minutes of work was to completely hose himself down at the dish sink, until he was so soaked that a manager offered him yet another free dry shirt.

I lost count of how many times he weaseled his way out of working a full shift, always claiming he felt sick from exertion.

One time, a bartender's friend drove by and took a picture of him sitting in the parking lot in an ambulance, wearing his uniform, and said, "Does this guy work with you?"

Define "work."

"Why do I have to prep more burgers? You gotta stop selling this shit so fast."

- *a prep cook with serious misconceptions about how restaurants work*

The Crazy Prep Cook

I always thought prepping looked easy and relaxing. I mean, how hard can it be to come in, read your list, listen to music as you complete your list, and leave?

Harder than it looks, I guess.

Our cook always prepped whatever she wanted. Screw that list the manager made for her last night. She'd prep three times the amount of something we never sold and let it rot, then not enough of something we sold every night.

I can't tell you how sick I was of telling customers, "No, sorry, we're out of pico de gallo for your chips. And shredded cheese for your nachos. Oops, and no more sauce for your dessert, either."

When she wasn't outside smoking four packs a day, she was cackling, rasping, and shrieking through the morning shifts, annoying me with every syllable she uttered. She'd then throw her unwashed equipment in the back sink, where a cook would have to haul it out of the way after she left, cussing her out the entire time.

Repeat the experience every shift for the rest of your employment.

Managing the Managers

Don't bite the hand that feeds you

"Want to see a
video of my cats?"

- *a misplaced cat lady, somehow managing a sports bar*

The Blasé General Manager

My GM was a nice, quiet, as non-confrontational as they come woman only a couple years older than me, who loved her husband, her cats, and quiet nights at home baking. Sometimes she'd bring in the results of hours in the confectioner's oven, and we'd all swoon over cookies, cupcakes, and elaborate candied apples.

If she wasn't talking about baking, she was showing you a cat video.

She always gave me the time off that I requested and we had a good relationship, but her placid nature didn't lend itself well to dealing with irate customers and bratty kitchen boys. She was timid about putting misbehaving employees back in their place, often saying how she wished she were in bed with her cats at 9 p.m. instead of at work.

I wondered why she stayed in a position so seemingly ill-suited for her, when she could open her own bakery or something. I guess you've got to pay for the cat food somehow.

"I brought stuff
to make pancakes."

- *a much-appreciated fun manager*

The Fun Assistant Manager

You know those managers who bring in pancake batter and chocolate chips and maple syrup and their own speakers and basically throw a dance party in the kitchen while making everyone breakfast?

The ones who pick up a Red Bull for you before work and make a specialty pizza for you all to share?

The ones who let you leave in the middle of a shift without clocking out to go to Chipotle?

I love those ones.

We were blessed to have two such managers at my restaurant, who were always ready to make work more fun and reward good employees with freedoms and treats. They were friendly, approachable, funny, and pleasant to work under.

Be thankful if you've had a manager like this. Bonus points if they're also open for honest communication and don't make you feel insignificant. We need more managers who know how to manage and make work fun at the same time.

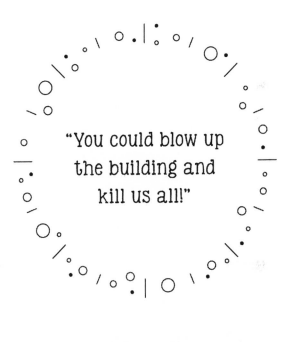

"You could blow up
the building and
kill us all!"

- an extremely unstable manager,
after I put sanitizer in the wrong bottle

The Hothead Slave Driver

Thank God this manager was only at my restaurant briefly as a fill-in, because I didn't sign up for the military.

Loud, bald, and red-faced, he kicked off our introductions by screaming at me when I tried to mix some soaps together to clean off a cutting board.

He'd walk around assigning cleaning tasks to the servers, as if there wasn't a full-time janitor employed six days a week (an insignificant detail, because he did absolutely nothing if the bathrooms were any indication). Most servers just sneered and walked away, but being the intimidated rule-follower that I once was, I quickly did my task so I could present it to him so I could leave without further interaction.

He later stepped down from management to date a bartender, and employees at every location breathed a collective sign of relief.

And so did our brand-new ticket machine. He'd broken the old one after a fit of fist-pounding, door-slamming, red-faced rage.

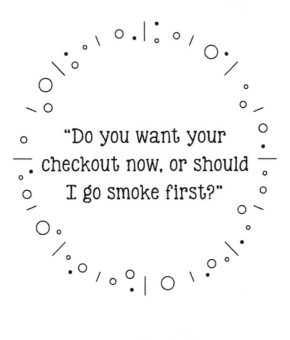

"Do you want your checkout now, or should I go smoke first?"

- a stoner shift supervisor

The Stoner

In the vein of the fun assistant manager was my oft-stoned shift supervisor, who cared as much about anything in that building as I cared to check the balance on someone's gift card.

With long hair, a backward baseball cap, and a blank look in his eyes, he spoke in a slow drawl that made me as unsure of what he was saying as he seemed to be. He mostly stayed in the kitchen because they needed as much help as they could get, and I'd yell for him to delete something occasionally or ask for my checkout. We could complain about the same things and people, and he kept me laughing with his dry, honest humor.

"Matt," I'd say, "you smell good. You smell kind of like my grandma when she used to smoke."

"Why'd she quit?" He paced back and forth.

"She died."

"So I smell like your dead grandma?"

Epilogue

If you made it to the end of this book, we must have a lot of life experiences in common.

Either that, or you actually thought some of this was funny.

No matter your role in a restaurant or the type of establishment you work in, be proud of your work and keep pushing forward.

Ignore the drama and the people who tell you to "get a real job."

Do what works best for you right now.

Do what will get you to living the life you ultimately want to live.

Thank you for sharing in my thoughts and laughter and annoyances in this industry.

Thank you for listening to my voice and lending your imagination to my experiences.

Thank you for the work you do.

Made in the USA
Monee, IL
23 November 2019